SandCastle™
Let's Measure

WHAT
in the
WORLD
is a
CUP?

Mary Elizabeth Salzmann

Consulting Editor, Diane Craig, M.A./Reading Specialist

ABDO
Publishing Company

Published by ABDO Publishing Company, 8000 West 78th Street, Edina, Minnesota 55439.
Copyright © 2009 by Abdo Consulting Group, Inc. International copyrights reserved in all countries.
No part of this book may be reproduced in any form without written permission from the publisher.
SandCastle™ is a trademark and logo of ABDO Publishing Company.

Printed in the United States.

Editor: Pam Price
Curriculum Coordinator: Nancy Tuminelly
Cover and Interior Design and Production: Colleen Dolphin, Mighty Media
Photo Credits: BananaStock Ltd., Colleen Dolphin, Shutterstock
Illustrations: Colleen Dolphin

The following manufacturers/names appearing in this book are trademarks:
Gold Medal® Flour, Pyrex® Glassware, Quaker Oats,® Sun-Maid® Raisins

Library of Congress Cataloging-in-Publication Data

Salzmann, Mary Elizabeth, 1968-

What in the world is a cup? / Mary Elizabeth Salzmann.

p. cm. -- (Let's measure)

ISBN 978-1-60453-162-6

1. Volume (Cubic content)--Juvenile literature. 2. Measurement--Juvenile literature.
3. Weights and measures--Juvenile literature. 4. Measuring instruments--Juvenile literature. I. Title.

QC104.S35 2009

530.8'13--dc22

2008005482

SandCastle™ books are created by a professional team of educators, reading specialists, and content developers around five essential components—phonemic awareness, phonics, vocabulary, text comprehension, and fluency— to assist young readers as they develop reading skills and strategies and increase their general knowledge. All books are written, reviewed, and leveled for guided reading, early reading intervention, and Accelerated Reader® programs for use in shared, guided, and independent reading and writing activities to support a balanced approach to literacy instruction. The SandCastle™ series has four levels that correspond to early literacy development in young children. The levels are provided to help teachers and parents select appropriate books for young readers.

SandCastle Level: Fluent

Emerging Readers
(no flags)

Beginning Readers
(1 flag)

Transitional Readers
(2 flags)

Fluent Readers
(3 flags)

SandCastle™ would like to hear from you! Please send us your comments or questions.

sandcastle@abdopublishing.com

www.abdopublishing.com

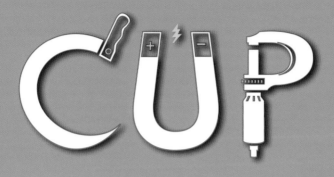

A cup is a unit
of measurement.
A juice glass holds
about 1 cup.

Cups are used to measure volume. When you know how much a cup is, you can find out how much of something there is.

The abbreviation for cup is c.

1 cup is the same as 1 c.

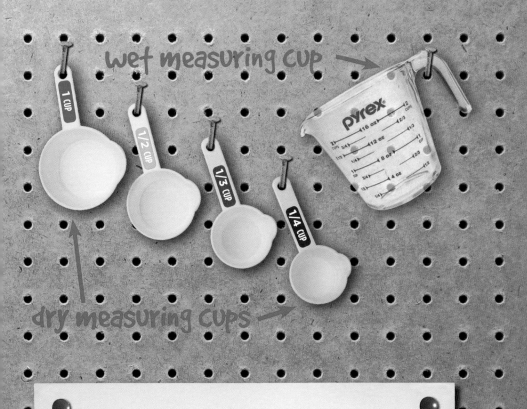

wet measuring cup →

dry measuring cups →

The tools you use to measure cups are called measuring cups. You measure liquids with a wet measuring cup. You measure solids with a dry measuring cup.

SOPHIA CAN MEASURE!

Sophia and her friend Kate measure in cups when they help Sophia's dad bake.

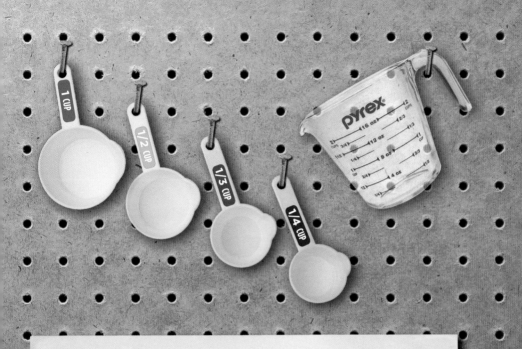

They need to make cookies, cupcakes, and an apple pie for a party.

For oatmeal raisin cookies, Sophia measures 3 cups of oatmeal.

Then she measures 1 cup of raisins.

For cupcakes, Sophia measures 2 cups of flour.

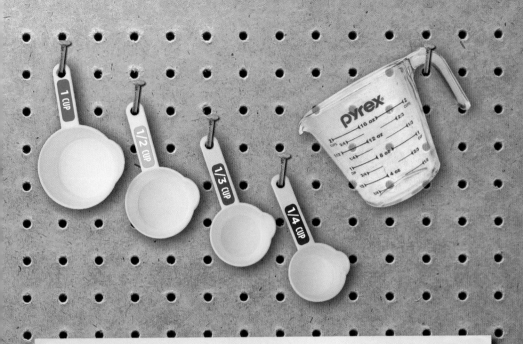

Then she measures 1 cup of milk.

Sophia measures 3 cups of flour for the pie crust.

She measures 6 cups of apple slices for the pie filling.

MEASURING EVERY DAY!

Jesse measures 1 cup of detergent when he helps do the laundry.

Laundry Detergent

Rebecca uses 3 cups of flour when she helps make pancakes for breakfast.

Steven feeds his dog 2 cups of dog food every day.

Hailey wonders how many cups of water fit in her beach pail. She counts each cup that she puts in the pail until it is full. Her pail holds 4 cups of water!

MEASURING IS FUN!

How many cups does it take to fill up your bathroom sink? What else can you measure in cups?

LET'S MEASURE!

Which of these things is about one cup?

(answer: coffee cup)

MORE ABOUT MEASURING

Volume

16 cups = 1 gallon

Sometimes you use part of a cup or gallon to measure something.

The recipe needs 1 and 1/2 cups of brown sugar.

We bought a half gallon of milk at the store.

GLOSSARY

crust – the pastry shell under and sometimes over a pie.

cupcake – a small cake about the size and shape of a teacup.

detergent – special soap used to wash clothes or dishes.

filling – a substance used to fill something.

laundry – clothes that have been or are being washed.

measurement – a piece of information discovered by measuring.

oatmeal – oats that have been ground up or flattened into flakes.

raisin – a dried grape.

slice – a thin piece cut from something.

unit – a definite quantity used as a standard of measurement.